2—

AUDREY

HEPBURN

An Audrey Hepburn

Biography

Katy Holborn

Table of Contents

Audrey Hepburn – The Fairest of Them All

Audrey Hepburn, the Icon

What makes an icon?

An icon is the definitive symbol of something relevant, captured in a representative image. It comes from the Greek *eikon* – a likeness. It is recognizable and distinct, and usually points to something sought or desired. It is an effort to condense an idea, so that one look is all it takes for something to almost immediately be grasped and understood.

An anonymous, ordinary man with a bag of groceries stands defiantly before tanks of the People's Liberation Army in Tiananmen

Square, China. Four soldiers struggle to raise a U.S. flag in Iwo Jima during World War II. African American athletes raise their black-gloved fists at the medal ceremony of the 1968 Summer Olympics. A handsome Marxist revolutionary looks on with burning eyes, his dark hair wavy beneath a signature, starred beret. A disheveled genius playfully sticks out his tongue for a photo. In entertainment, a blond bombshell stands above the subway grates of New York City, and her flowing white skirt flies up with the wind – a strong case for why gentlemen should prefer blondes.

The latter, Marilyn Monroe, is as distinct and unforgettable a Hollywood icon as they come. She is perhaps, *The* Hollywood Icon. But her foil, a tall, slim, gamine ingénue, had her own mark to make in Tinsel Town – for who could forget the waifish Audrey Hepburn in a trim, black Givenchy dress, covered to the elbows in gloves, and thick ropes of pearls adorning her long, slim neck? This is Hepburn at her chic, most memorable best, in character as Holly Golightly, the charming but troubled New York socialite from the film, *Breakfast at Tiffany's* (1961).

It is unjust but irresistible to pit these two women together. Indeed, if later revelations hold true, Audrey Hepburn's most iconic role and unforgettable image might have actually been meant for Marilyn Monroe herself. Writer Truman Capote, on whose story the movie was based, had known the blond bombshell and is said to have wanted Monroe for the role of Holly. Monroe and Golightly, after all, had much more in common – Holly Golightly the character is the reinvention of a Texan vagrant named Lulamae Barnes, not at all unlike Marilyn Monroe's real past as Norma Jeane Baker. But for better or worse (for we will now never know), the role was won by Audrey Hepburn and she had owned it so completely that we can no longer imagine anyone else inhabiting that compelling character as if it were a second skin. Audrey Hepburn and Holly Golightly became intertwined, and cinema and ideals of beauty would never be the same again.

Marilyn Monroe and Audrey Hepburn's iconic, public images are easy to compare because they are almost polar opposites. There's the blonde in the flowing white dress with her playful, mature sexuality. On the other side, an almost childlike brunette restrained in chic, tailored black. Both women are breathtakingly, unforgettably beautiful in each of their own ways and any woman in the world can aspire to be either one of them. But history would show it is the sultry blonde who actually had an innocent, childlike vulnerability, while the slender brunette was the one with the steely strength. She was, after all, among many other things, a fundraiser and courier for the Dutch resistance during World War II – and she was only in her early teens at the time!

Audrey Hepburn died more than twenty years ago, of cancer in 1993. But her doe eyes continue to stare at us and seemingly look through us across time and space, immortalized and beloved by film. The camera, moving or otherwise, loved her and the light always found her, even from beneath the wide brims of her stiff, chic hats.

Her appeal cuts across genders and across generations. Her sense of style is immortal; at the very least, she helped place a little black dress in every girl's closet. She still sends women of all ages into Tiffany's in New York City, each one hoping to invoke her effortless, timeless, aristocratic style. Even women who have never seen any of her movies would be able to recognize the gamine woman in the pearls and the black dress. Even women who do not know her name could find in her an aspiration. An ideal.

She is a beacon of enviable style, sure, but clothing is just one part of her iconography. It must be remembered that in *Breakfast at Tiffany's*, she is as captivating in an LBD as she is in a man's white tuxedo shirt and an ostentatious eye mask. She simply had that mysterious X-factor, an irresistible inner light. She had carriage and grace. She had charm and easy humor. She had intelligence and warmth.

These are just a few of the things that makes a star like Audrey Hepburn transcend the movies to icon-status. She wasn't just beautiful; so many women, especially in her field, are beautiful. More than that, she became the symbol for an ideal of timeless relevance - that is, what it means to be a woman of style and substance. It was beyond beauty. It was a way of life and being.

Life Before Hollywood

Audrey Hepburn's most memorable works were about the power of transformation.

In *Breakfast at Tiffany's*, she sparkled as Holly Golightly, the scheming, charming, glamorous incarnation of an ambitious woman who would have otherwise simply been an ordinary little Lulamae Barnes with a quiet life in Texas. As Jo Stockton in *Funny Face* (1957), she is an intellectual snob, a hipster even before hipsters were a thing, turning from bookish to stylish thanks to a fashion editor with guts and a vision, and a photographer who steals her heart. In *Sabrina* (1954), she is the titular character, Sabrina Fairchild, caught between the affections of the two Larrabee brothers. The chauffeur's once-naive daughter, long ignored, deftly secures the affections of both men after a Paris makeover. In *Roman Holiday* (1953), for which Hepburn won a coveted Academy Award, she flips the script and goes from Princess Ann to commoner in disguise (still gorgeous and genteel, however), changing her hair and stealing away for a day of normalcy, freedom and romance. In *My Fair Lady* (1964), she goes for the full *Pygmalion* treatment as Eliza Doolittle, spunky, flower seller with a Cockney accent, subject to a bet that turns her into a lady of upper-class speech and fine manners.

She shone in these roles probably because she had a gift for transformation in real life. In her work as an entertainer, she shifted from stage actress to screen star and she would collect accolades wherever she went, as if it were so easy. Few in her field could match her Emmy, Grammy, Oscar and Tony wins. But beyond the entertainment industry, she would also wear many hats. She was a child working for the Dutch resistance during World War II, and had likely honed some of her acting skills there, in concealing not only her British citizenship and rearing, but also her dangerous secrets. She was a dancer and chorus girl before she made the graceful leap to acting on Broadway and in Hollywood. Near the end of her life, she would hang up the acting cap and take on the cause of children in landmark philanthropic work for UNICEF, which would eventually inspire more of her fellow entertainers to use their fame and influence for the greater good. She was a global citizen before it was cool.

Throughout all these changes, she was a woman always in motion but poised and held together by a calm sense of self, like the eye of a storm.

Edda Kathleen van Heemstra Hepburn-Ruston - Audrey Hepburn as she would eventually be known - was born a British citizen on the 4th of May, 1929, in Brussels, Belgium. Her father, Joseph Anthony Ruston, was born of privilege in Bohemia (a region later absorbed into the current Czech Republic) to an English father and a German mother. Like many aristocrats of his time, Joseph went to private school, spoke several languages and was a gifted horseman. He worked for the British diplomatic service, at which capacity he spent time on assignment in the Dutch East Indies. He found his first love there, but would eventually divorce her to marry a Dutch baroness, Ella van Heemstra. Van Heemstra, whom Ruston wed in 1926, was Audrey Hepburn's mother. Joseph and Ella moved to Brussels when he was working for a merchant company expanding operations out from London. Audrey was thus a British citizen born in Belgium. The family – Joseph, Ella, Audrey and two sons from the baroness' previous marriage, Alexander and Jan - would settle there.

The years between the end of World War I in 1918 and the start of World War II in 1939, was a time of rapid change in Europe. In Italy and Germany, Fascism – a political ideology characterized by intense nationalism, obedience to an all-powerful state, and focus on the needs of the community over that of the individual – was on the rise. In these interwar years, this particular brand of politics also entailed the buildup of military strength, the subjugation of groups or races deemed inferior, and the expansion of territory or reclamation of old (sometimes even mythic) territory, to promote or restore national grandeur and pride.

Ambitious, intelligent and charismatic men knew how to craft and deliver messages that would resonate with a dissatisfied people. Propaganda was paramount, and would bring popular support behind authoritarian leaders like Italian dictator Benito Musolini and the German fuhrer, Adolf Hitler. By May of 1939, Mussolini and Hitler would be formally allied in their shared objectives via the "Pact of Steel." Just a few months after that, in September, the German invasion of Allied country, Poland, prompted Britain and France to declare war on Germany. It was the start of the Second World War, though the events leading up to it, including the conclusion of the First World War and the infamously harsh measures imposed upon Germany for reparations as a result of it, have been in motion for years.

This is the scenario in which the young family found themselves. In its popularity, fascism could even manage to capture the support of Audrey Hepburn's mother and father, and in effect, link them with the Nazis.

When Audrey Hepburn's Hollywood star rose after World War II, her handlers and industry spin doctors found good cause to lionize her war efforts – but they had just as many incentives to closet away the family's links to the movement championed by the Axis powers. This means that some information are unconfirmed or inconsistent across sources, and are publicly revealed late, if they are ever revealed at all. Accounts vary, but reports would later come out that one or both of Audrey Hepburn's parents have participated in fundraisers for British fascism, and Joseph in particular may have been prominent enough within the movement to have shared a meal with Adolf Hitler in Munich along with a British fascist figure that he supported. Reports state he would even be sent to prison for a time, for his involvement in fascist activities.

But before that, for unknown reasons, Joseph left Ella and the family when Audrey was only six years old in 1935. Divorce came later when she was nine. It may have been because he tired of Ella's strong will. It may have also been because they differed in opinions and argued frequently, especially with Ella reportedly being more and more discomfited by Hitler's rise to power.

Whatever the reason for the family's breaking, Joseph lived in London where he added "Hepburn" to his name. The surname came from his mother's side and carried some prestige, but he may have also included it to seem more British as the lines in Europe began to be drawn leading up to the war. He wasn't quite in his immediate family's life at this time, but he was able to see Audrey occasionally there, as she attended a boarding school in Kent.

Joseph, like his ex-wife Ella, wasn't a particularly affectionate parent, but Audrey was a devoted daughter and open about her adoration for her father. She had actually advocated to continue to see him. By some accounts, he also showed continuing care for her welfare when, at the start of the Second World War, he reportedly bore his daughter away from Britain and brought her to her mother in the Netherlands, which was a neutral country. Other reports, however, say it was Audrey's mother Ella who had moved her back, hoping Holland's neutrality would spare the family from the ravages of war. Either way, at the outbreak of World War II,

Audrey was settled in Arnhem in Holland, in the false hope that it would be safer. The move started well enough, with Audrey able to pursue her education and study ballet.

While at school in London, she was shy and on the chubby side, making her the target of teasing in school. In Holland's Conservatory of Music and Dance, however, she enrolled, studied dance, and began to bloom. But Holland wouldn't be an untouched refuge for very long.

Despite the Netherlands' neutral standing, it was occupied by Nazi Germany in 1940. Audrey continued with her training in the arts, but few things stayed the same. Food was rationed and even then, there was little guarantee of getting anything. Fuel and heating were scarce too, but these were nothing compared to the images of violence she as a child caught in the war, would be subject to. There were men shot and killed on the streets. There was constant fear and uncertainty. As they did in other countries, Hitler's soldiers targeted Jews here too, and even got their tentacles into a few members of the Van Heemstra family, who had some Jewish ancestry.

In occupied Holland, Ella and her children did what they could to defy their occupiers and survive the war. Audrey's mother tried to pass as pro-German, but much of their valuables and properties would still be taken from them. One of her older brothers would be rounded up for a grueling labor camp; the other would go underground to avoid the same fate.

Audrey had her own part to play, too. Make that several parts to play. She was barely in her teens but she put her talents to good use, dancing in so-called "blackout performances." These were quiet shows behind closed doors and shuttered windows to no applause, so that they would not be discovered by the Germans as they raised funds for the Dutch Resistance and hid the money in their ballet shoes. She helped spread literature against the Nazis, became a child courier for the Resistance, and was reportedly in contact with downed Allied pilots secreted in Dutch homes, serving as messenger and delivering food. She also snuck in a few secret dance lessons for younger students, so that she could earn extra money for her family.

As the war raged on and the Germans crawled to a defeat, food became even scarcer. The diet comprised of diluted soup, improvised bread and sometimes even grass. Audrey suffered malnutrition and even had to stop dancing for a time. She shrank to less than 90 lbs., and had spells of other diseases. She would carry the effects of that difficult time in her body for ever afterwards – because that distinct waif attractiveness she would be known for had been carved by changes in her metabolism.

Thankfully, Audrey Hepburn would survive everything the Second World War threw at her, and so would her family. Even her half-brothers, including the one sent away to a labor camp, would find their way home a few weeks after the arrival of the Allied troops and the defeat of the Nazis in 1945.

The Start of a Career

During the war, Audrey Hepburn's love of
the arts and performing helped carry her
through tough times. It wasn't just that it
helped her raise funds for her family and the
Dutch resistance, it was also expression, and
the normalcy of training while the world
seemed to be falling all around her. After the
war, she and her mother looked at dance in a
different way – it wasn't just a means of
surviving the present. It was also the path to
the future.

Ella brought Audrey to Amsterdam, in the
sphere of Dutch ballet legend Sonia Gaskell.
Payment for the rigorous training would
have been hard to come by, if Gaskell
reportedly hadn't decided to give Audrey a
chance to learn. By 1946, she was dancing at

the Hortus Theater under the eagle-eye of critics. A couple of years later, she made her way to London to study at the prestigious Marie Rambert Ballet School. Funds were still tight, and for a time she had to put off enrollment. But eventually, between Audrey and her mother, they found ways to make it work. Ella was employed in a miscellany of jobs, including managing flats. Audrey did modeling work, and was again helped along by her teacher. Rambert even took her in for a few months.

Her ballet teachers must have seen some potential in her, but Audrey was also realistic about her prospects. She recognized her own limitations, and started to divert her ambitions to other forms of performing. She joined the chorus line of *High Button Shoes* for almost 300 performances. In 1949, she would be part of musical revue *Sauce Tartare* for hundreds of shows too, and *Sauce Piquante* after it. She also managed to land small parts in film and television, including *Young Wives' Tale* (1951) and *The Lavender Hill Mob* (1951).

The hardworking performer went from role to role, and eventually one part led to another, as if each one was a section of pavement winding its way to Hollywood.

In 1951, while in production for *The Secret People*, she secured a spot in *Nous Irons A Monte Carlo*. The shoot for the latter brought her to film in the French Riviera, which in turn brought her into the path of French writer Colette – who fancied she may have found in Audrey Hepburn, the titular character, *Gigi* for its adaptation as a play on

Broadway. That same year, Audrey would blow away William Wyler at a screen test and make her first step in conquering Hollywood. She was testing for *Roman Holiday* (1953).

Hollywood's Golden Girl

The kidnapping of Jaycee Lee Dugard in 1991 remains one of the highest profile kidnappings in history. In 1991, eleven-year-old Dugard was taken by Phillip and Nancy Garrido from the streets of her hometown in California. She spent eighteen years in captivity, during which time she was raped repeatedly and gave birth to two daughters, before being freed after Phillip and Nancy Garrido's arrest in 2009.

Audrey Hepburn was signed up for a Broadway play and a Hollywood movie. *Gigi* was a hit, and Audrey was considered a success in it. She struggled at the start, but improved through vocal coaching and hard work. She would continue to study and hone her craft even after *Gigi*'s success, at the Tarassova School of Ballet in Manhattan.

But her career wasn't the only thing going well for the gamine beauty. Audrey Hepburn in 1951 was successful and also in love.

Her first serious relationship had been a short-lived one with Marcel le Bon, when she and the French singer / lyricist were in *Sauce Piquante*. Le Bon was followed by multimillionaire James Hanson, who was an industrialist and whose family was in the trucking business. They started a relationship after production for *The Lavender Hill Mob* in 1949. When she did *Gigi* in 1951, it was fortunate that his work sometimes took him to New York (aside from Britain and Canada), and they managed to see a lot of each other during this period.

He would even put a diamond engagement ring on her finger in 1951. It must have been a heady time alongside all of her success, but by 1952, the demands of her rising career began to take a toll on their relationship. Immediately after *Gigi* – as in, on closing night! - she headed to Italy for the filming of *Roman Holiday*. The wedding with Hanson, planned for the Spring after *Gigi* but before her work began for *Roman Holiday*, was postponed. When her *Roman Holiday* filming ended, however, she plunged right into a road tour for *Gigi* in America, and there was yet another wedding postponement. Eventually, she and Hanson split. She wanted to give proper time for the man who would be her husband, which the demands of her job would not have been able to allow at that point of the career she had worked so hard to achieve.

Audrey Hepburn may have lost Hanson, but she gained the love of critics and audiences alike, when *Roman Holiday* came out in 1953. She wasn't just a fresh-faced beauty, another one of Hollywood's fine young things of the moment. She also had 'It.' She knew how to carry clothes and the fashion industry was also starting to pay attention.

It certainly helped that she was also a force to be reckoned with in acting. As a matter of fact, her star-making turn in *Roman Holiday* – her first major role, really, would help her nab an Academy Award for best actress in March of 1954.

Her *Roman Holiday* triumph was just the beginning for Hollywood's delightful ingénue. By 1953 she was filming *Sabrina* in Long Island, New York with William Holden and Humphrey Bogart as the wealthy Larrabee brothers vying for the affections of the chauffeur's fetching daughter, under the direction of Billy Wilder. If *Roman Holiday* helped Hepburn catch the attention of eagle-eyed fashion aficionados everywhere, *Sabrina* was where she would make a bold and conscious, indelible mark on the industry.

Paramount's famous wardrobe supervisor, Edith Head, was responsible for Audrey Hepburn's stunning turn as Princess Ann in *Roman Holiday*. In *Sabrina*, however, the wardrobe supervisor's services would only be used for a few ensembles in the film, and not particularly significant ones at that. Such a job would instead fall upon the shoulders of a young French design sensation named Hubert de Givenchy, who was only 26 years old at the time. The idea of using genuine French couture purchased in Paris for use in the movie was reportedly Hepburn's. She was a lover of fashion, and had once described it as so much of a passion that it was *"practically a vice."*

Givenchy and Hepburn were brought together by Gladys de Segonzac of Schiaparelli, and wife of the head of Paramount in Paris. At the time, *Roman Holiday* wasn't released yet and Givenchy wouldn't have known much (if anything at all) about the persuasive waif knocking on his door and seeking his services. But she explained her purpose to the hot young couturier of the moment, and though he was hesitant due to workloads for an upcoming collection, he let the winsome ingénue try on a few sample clothes that he had in his atelier. They were from the previous season, but the ecstatic Hepburn all but transformed before their very eyes in Givenchy's fashions. Givenchy would later describe Audrey as having the ability to give life to clothes. They became fast friends and would work together not only for seven more movie projects, but he would also dress her in her personal life. They were both disciplined and hard-working and certainly did a lot of business together, but they were more like brother and sister. He was her beloved confidant, privy to the most intimate parts of her life, including details of her romantic entanglements and later, even her will.

Billy Wilder approved of Hepburn's choices for *Sabrina*, but as filming progressed, became all the more rapturous of his lead actress' radiance in signature Givenchy. Scenes of the movie seemed to weave outwards from how Hepburn looked, affecting how they were shot and edited, and even affecting how some of the encounters between characters were re-written. Audrey was simply captivating, and would even ensnare the real-life affections of her co-star, the married and 11-years older, William Holden (the affair wouldn't get very far, but more on the loves of Audrey Hepburn, later).

In *Sabrina*, Hepburn showed that she knew what she wanted for a role. She knew what she wanted in a designer. She had an understanding not only of her own preferences, but also what looked good on her. She was detail-oriented and wasn't afraid of infusing a look with quirk and character. She was only in her 20's and a Hollywood newbie, but she already had a distinctive sense of style. That style flowed from and into her and her character fluidly, such that sometimes, it was hard to tell where off-screen Audrey Hepburn started and where the on-screen character began.

When the film opened in the United States in 1954, it was well received. But Audrey, in particular, was described ecstatically. Critics called her magical, beguiling, bewitching – as if she were a rare, otherworldly creature of legend and fairy tale which, in a way, she was.

Sabrina fever – or perhaps, Audrey fever? – wasn't just sweeping across America. Premieres and live appearances by the star sent the fan frenzy across the seas, too. In the Netherlands, where the premiere was also a homecoming for Audrey in late 1954, there were modeling shows for Givenchy and signing events which helped raise funds for Dutch veterans. In France in early 1955, promotions around the premiere were focused on the film's links to French fashion.

While *Sabrina* was a big commercial and critical success and she seemed confident, however, Audrey Hepburn could be very critical of her own work. She had once been horrified at the kind of salary her acting performances could command, a salary that would eventually catapult her into being among the highest-paid actors in the globe.

She was uncomfortable with it and felt unworthy. Her acting insecurities was also probably why she paid so much attention to wardrobe, aside from her sheer love of fashion; she used her character's clothes to tell a story, allowing her to flesh out a role and help improve her dramatic technique.

Why she should have been worried so much about her acting prowess is a mystery. Her performance in *Sabrina* got her another Academy Award nomination in 1955, though she would lose this race to Grace Kelly's *A Country Girl*. If she had any more reservations after that, one would think that the other critical successes of her career would be some balm to her acting insecurities. Over the course of her career in film, television and stage, she would garner multiple nominations and wins from various prestigious bodies. The Academy Awards would nominate her as Best Actress in a Leading Role for *The Nun's Story* (1959), *Breakfast at Tiffany's* (1961) and *Wait Until Dark*, (1967). The Golden Globes would honor her too, with a Best Actress-Drama win for *Roman Holiday* (1953), and nominations for her acting work in the same films as that mentioned in the Academy Awards list above, plus for her work in *War and Peace* (1956), *Love in the Afternoon*, (1957), *Charade* (1963), *My Fair Lady* (1964), and *Two for the Road* (1967). Various projects would also gather recognition from the Primetime Emmy Awards, the BAFTAs, the Screen Actors Guild Awards, the Grammy's, and the New York Film Critics Circle.

Outside of film and television, Audrey Hepburn would also find recognition for her work on the stage. In 1954, she starred in *Ondine* on Broadway, and walked away with a Best Stage Actress Tony award for her efforts. She was starring opposite one Mr. Mel Ferrer, at the time.

Audrey in Love

Audrey Hepburn was a lovely woman with so much to offer. Beauty, intelligence, discipline, manners, talent, affection... the list could go on and on. She was forgiving and admiring of her father, even after Joseph left the family. Hubert de Givenchy had fond memories of getting simple phone calls where the superstar would just express her love of the man who helped forge her style and whom she considered a brother. She was a good daughter, who helped provide for her family during the war, and would continue to offer them support when she found success as an actress. Even her estranged and eventually remarried father, who settled quietly in Dublin, Ireland later in life, would get both correspondence as well as financial support from Audrey. So how could she have been as a girlfriend and wife? What would it have been like, for a man to be lucky enough to have those signature doe-eyes looking at him, and only him, with such sparkling, cinematic love and longing?

At this point, we already know that Audrey reportedly had a short-lived romance with fellow stage performer, Marcel le Bon. He was soon followed by wealthy businessman James Hanson, with whom she split up amicably when it became clear that the demands of their careers seemed incompatible to keeping their love alive. They were so close to the altar that she already managed several wedding dress fittings with the sister designers, Fontana. The dress would (*of course!*) later be auctioned.

Eventually though, it would be one fairly controversial Mr. Mel Ferrer who would win the hand of the gamine superstar. They met at a party in London in 1953, around the time of the London premiere of *Roman Holiday*. Ferrer, an actor and director, wasn't quite the youth and stability of Audrey's previous love, James Hanson. At the time, Ferrer had been divorced twice, had several children, and was 12 years older than her. But they had chemistry, and sparks flew. Shortly after their fateful meeting, Ferrer sent her the script for a Broadway production of *Ondine*, and they both starred in the well-reviewed staging in February of 1954 after her work filming for *Sabrina* finished. Her time in *Ondine* would be cut short due to health problems, but what she showed on the stage was enough to secure her a Best Actress Tony award.

The show closed in July and Audrey worked on restoring her health, finding refuge in Switzerland. It was also where she and Mel married in September, 1954. They honeymooned in Italy where he was working, and in the Netherlands where she was promoting *Sabrina* and doing fundraisers for the League of Dutch Military War Invalids.

Audrey and Mel tried to make their marriage work. They did several projects together, and when their individual acting commitments took them to different locales, they hopped around from country to country just to see each other.

Hepburn and Ferrer were together in Italy for the filming of *War and Peace* (1956) and in Hollywood for *Green Mansions* (1958) and the television movie, *Mayerling* (1957). The projects were unfortunately poorly received, but the Ferrers never lacked for work and Audrey in particular had the pick of them; around this time, she would be doing *Funny Face* (1957) with Fred Astaire, as well as the high-grossing *The Nun's Story* (1959). Besides, the Ferrers had other concerns.

Audrey had a miscarriage in March, 1955. She suffered another such loss in 1959, shortly after a fall that broke her back while filming *The Unforgiven* (1960) in Mexico. When she got pregnant again, she resolved against taxing her body with the rigors of acting work until she gave birth. Her commitment to having a child had her turning down projects like *The West Side Story* and an Alfred Hitchcock film. Her next project would be after the birth of her and Mel's son, Sean, who was born in Lucerne, Switzerland in July, 1960.

After Sean's birth, she worked on a 'little' project called *Breakfast at Tiffany's* (1961), for which she would always be remembered and cherished by film and fashion fans everywhere. Few things could dim Audrey Hepburn's star after that – she shone even in small roles and flops. But one role would bring her criticism, that of the lead, Eliza Doolittle in *My Fair Lady*. The role was originated by a young and so wonderfully promising Julie Andrews on Broadway, but Andrews did not have the cachet yet in Hollywood for them to risk bringing her into the screens to play the part. The film had a big budget, and producers were not comfortable resting the film on a relative unknown's shoulders. Audrey Hepburn's efforts at a cockney accent would be panned, and though she did some singing, she was ultimately dubbed over by Marni Nixon. That year, the Academy Award did not bother with handing her a nomination. That year, the Best Actress Award went to Julie Andrews, as the titular role in *Mary Poppins*.

The Perks and Perils of Being a 'Mr. Hepburn?'

Being a mom barely slowed down the superstar's movie career, even though she prized her family above all else. Aside from *Breakfast at Tiffany's* and *My Fair Lady*, Audrey worked in other high-profile projects; with *Roman Holiday*'s William Wyler again, for *The Children's Hour*; with her *Sabrina* co-star William Holden in *Paris When It Sizzles*; and with *Roman Holiday* leading man, Cary Grant in the hit, *Charade*. Mel Ferrer kept busy too, but his wife was clearly the bigger star. Then again, who could've been bigger than Audrey Hepburn at her peak then, when her residual light *now* can still outshine many of today's artists?

Inevitably, because husband and wife were in the same field and the disparity in their careers had the woman doing much better than the man, people theorized that such a reversal in power dynamics can create strain in a marriage. He could be domineering and controlling to her too, some observers noted. While it couldn't have been easy being regarded as 'Mr. Hepburn' and Ferrer had to find ways to assert himself, however, he always did say he preferred being behind the scenes to acting and that it was unrealistic to compete with Hepburn, so perhaps it was a contributor to the failure of the marriage, but it wasn't the only one. Maybe it was actually because he wanted her to continue working in film, while she wanted to spend more time with family, as some reports suggest. At any rate, they always did have a complex

love story so probably, the eventual end of
their marriage was just as intricate, a mix of
several factors rather than just a single cause.

Melchor Gaston Ferrer was born in Elborn,
New Jersey in 1917, to a surgeon and a New
York socialite. His posh background, along
with his pricey private schooling and
attendance at Princeton, gave him an
aristocratic quality to match his dashing
looks. He was cosmopolitan and multi-
lingual. He didn't finish schooling in
Princeton, but did leave with the
Playwright's Award and ambitions of
becoming an actor. He fought his way to his
dreams, starting out as a chorus dancer on
Broadway and eventually landing small
roles in plays. He would also find work in
radio and as a producer and as a director. He
would straddle that line between being on

screen and being away from it all throughout his professional life, as he got more and more successful. His time in Broadway and Hollywood would be true to that pattern, of acting in one project and directing or producing another. He also co-founded La Jolla Playhouse in California.

Indeed, over the course of his career, he would have over 100 film and television credits under his belt, for acting work and for work behind-the-scenes. His acting is best remembered for compelling roles in *Lili* (1953), where he played an embittered puppeteer pining for Leslie Caron's title role; and in swashbuckler classic *Scaramouche* (1952) as the ruthless swordsman, Marquis de Maynes. In this movie, Ferrer as de Maynes played the villain in one of cinema history's greatest swordfights. It is an even more stunning feat, considering Ferrer had conquered mobility problems in his arm after catching polio earlier in his career.

He would also be remembered for directing Audrey in the unfortunate *Green Mansions* (1959). It was a big flop in her otherwise stellar career. He should, however, also be remembered for steering Audrey toward her Tony Award-winning Broadway role in *Ondine* in 1954, and for the hit *Wait Until Dark* (1967), which he produced. Hepburn would get her fifth and final Best Actress Academy award nomination for her role in that film.

Mel Ferrer would find love with four women in five marriages over the course of his life. He married Frances Pilchard twice, with Barbara Tripp in between their two marriages. He had children with both women, and was still married when he met Audrey Hepburn at a party in 1953.

Ferrer and Hepburn had immediate chemistry, but chemistry alone does not make a lasting relationship. He was married, had children, was much older, and was not quite approved by Hepburn's mother, the baroness Ella van Heemstra. The relationship wouldn't go far and soon, Hepburn would be in the sphere of handsome, notorious Hollywood playboy, William Holden.

Holden and Hepburn were co-stars in *Sabrina*. They were filming in New York and became allies in a tense set, where pressure on the Hollywood newbie was high, on top of all of them having to contend with the brooding but gifted veteran, Humphrey

Bogart. Bogart was much older than Holden and Hepburn, and was reportedly skeptical of Holden's acting skills, felt threatened by Holden's rapport and work history with director Billy Wilder, and was uncomfortable in the romantic comedy genre, which was a departure from his usual fare. In this environment, Holden and Hepburn reportedly connected and fell passionately in love. Ardis, Holden's tolerant wife who let her notorious husband have a long romantic leash, met Audrey over dinner and knew she had a genuine rival who was not at all like Holden's previous, passing flings. After that meeting, she allegedly asked her husband to interact with Audrey only in a professional capacity, but he wouldn't have it. What would eventually end the affair, however, was that Audrey reportedly wanted to have children badly, while Holden, who had a vasectomy, could no longer provide. The relationship ended in heartbreak, especially for Holden who would resort to reckless behavior and drinking to such a self-destructive level that when he worked with Audrey again for *Paris When It Sizzles* in 1962, he looked more haggard and eventually had to go to rehab.

Not that Audrey Hepburn would have been free to pursue a love affair with Holden when they reunited to film *Paris When It Sizzles*. By that time, she was already long married to Mel Ferrer, who made a comeback in Audrey's life after her romance with Holden fell apart and Ferrer had acquired his third divorce in 1954. That year, they worked on the successful *Ondine* on

Broadway, and would marry shortly afterwards.

The marriage wouldn't last for very long. Their union would suffer the same fate as that of Ferrer's previous other walks down the aisle - divorce. Allegedly, aside from the strain the disparity in their careers may have contributed to the crumbling of their marriage, Ferrer was also somewhat neurotic and overprotective. He controlled interactions with his wife, secreted away her phone number, and was often her spokesman. The term "Svengali" would be mentioned a few times regarding Mel Ferrer's handling of Audrey Hepburn, after the fictional villain of the 1894 novel *Trilby* by George du Maurier. Svengali puts model Trilby under his spell, turning her into a star but manipulating her and keeping control of her.

These are accusations Hepburn would laughingly brush off, and some of Ferrer's defenders say it was also Hepburn's way to defer to her husband anyway. At any rate, it is inconclusive whether or not this dynamic contributed to the end of their marriage, for Audrey wouldn't say bad things about Mel Ferrer afterwards, nor would he do the same of her. It probably didn't help them though, that much of her and Ferrer's film work together, with the exception of *Wait Until Dark*, were not being received well by audiences and/or critics either.

Another factor that could have contributed to the dissolution of the marriage was that Mel Ferrer allegedly had girlfriends ... Not that the revered Hepburn was completely saintly. If rumors are true, Hepburn may have also indulged in a few extramarital romances of her own, such as one with screenwriter Robert Anderson during the filming of *The Nun's Story* in 1957, or one with *Two for the Road* (1967) co-star Albert Finney. Ferrer and Hepburn began living separately in 1967, and announced their divorce in 1968 after 14 years of marriage and one son, Sean Hepburn-Ferrer. Sean went to Audrey's custody.

Mel Ferrer continued to work in various projects after the split, with fans able to spot him in American television shows like *Falcon Crest*, *Fantasy Island* and *Murder, She Wrote*, and a few other projects from nations as varied as France, Germany, Italy and Spain. He and Audrey would speak extremely sporadically after their marriage ended, with some reports saying they spoke as little as twice over 25 years. He was visibly shaken by her death, however, reportedly weeping openly in her funeral and needing comfort from the son they shared, Sean. Ferrer outlived Hepburn by many years, and passed away at age 90 in Santa Barbara, California in 2008. At the time of his death, he was married to Beligian, Elizabeth Soukhotine, whom he wedded in 1971.

Audrey as a Mother

The 1968 divorce between Ferrer and
Hepburn was hard on the couple's son, Sean.
It was already difficult being the only child
of two stars; when they were busy jetting
around the world for work, he would often
end up with his grandmother and his nanny.
But Mel and Audrey tried not to fight in
front of him even at the height of their
troubles, and they did whatever they could
to assure Sean that he was loved and that the
fracture of their family was through no fault
of his. They also did not put him in the
middle of their troubles, by refraining from
saying anything bad about each other. Later,
Audrey Hepburn would say that sometimes,
the relationship between two good, loving

people just doesn't survive a difficult situation even if you try and try.

Sean loved both of his parents. He would have fond remembrances of his mother being silly, and telling him stories or nursing him through illness. She would sometimes surprise Sean's visiting friends by her normalcy, wearing an apron and preparing a meal. Sean and Audrey were close, and after he was born she took on less acting work even if the parts and offers continued to come. Audrey always wanted children and a family, and she was clear on her priorities at that point of her life.

She went into semi-retirement, and found love anew in her second and final marriage, to Italian psychiatrist / neurologist Dr. Andrea Dotti in 1969 whom she met at a private cruise. She was prioritizing her family at this point, and had reportedly been wanting a quiet life being a doctor's wife. They settled in Rome with Sean, but she kept a home in Switzerland, managed by her mother who also resided there. The marriage between Dotti and Hepburn produced another son for Audrey, Luca Dotti, in 1970. At that point, she was 40 and was by all accounts a supermom, cooking meals and walking her children to school.

By many accounts, it was hard to drag her back into the movie business. She had reportedly asked not to be sent scripts as early as 1967. According to Terrance Young, with whom Audrey worked in the hit, *Wait Until Dark*, getting her into a project included an intricate wooing that involved getting her to even entertain the possibility of returning to film work; then getting her to actually read a script; then pitching her on how good it is; then convincing her being away for a few weeks wouldn't be detrimental to her kids; then talking about things like her cherished topic of costumes; and then, *then* one was still likely to get a 'no thank you.'

Few things would draw her out of the relatively quiet family life she had fashioned for herself. Among them, charity work with UNICEF, and the high-profile film, *Robin and Marian* with Sean Connery. Film reviews were mixed when they came out, but as always, Audrey Hepburn was welcomed back and cherished. She would also make a few public appearances in the mid-1970s, including presenting the Best Picture Oscar in 1975 – for which she, in a fairly minor role as presenter, was actually given a standing ovation.

Even when she placed such a priority on her family though, her marriage still wouldn't work out. The doctor she married had reportedly been cavorting around with other women. The marriage ended after 13 years, as more and more reports of Dotti's scandalous activities hit the press. The Dotti divorce wouldn't be until 1982 but Audrey would be rumored to have an extramarital fling prior to that, with *Bloodline* co-star Ben Gazzara in 1979. Gazzara was also said to be in an unhappy marriage, a point of commonality for the co-stars. Aside from that rumored relationship, when the split with Dotti came along, Audrey was already in another, this time with Dutch businessman and actor, Robert Wolders.

Love at Last, Until the Last

Married twice, divorced twice.

But never was Audrey Hepburn without love.

The man with whom Audrey Hepburn spent the rest of her life was actually someone whom she never married: Robert Wolders. He was born the 28th of September, 1936 in the Netherlands, and was a Dutch businessman and actor. He was very handsome, known for his work in the hit series *Laredo*, for which he did 26 episodes in the 1960s. He was famously the widower of British-American actress Merle Oberon, so in some ways, he was used to being with a woman in the spotlight.

The exotic Merle Oberon, Wolders' first wife, is known for her dramatic beauty, which ranked among the best of Hollywood's Golden Age, even if her filmography wasn't quite filled with hits. She is best remembered for her role as the heroine in William Wyler's adaptation of *Wuthering Heights* (1939), where she starred alongside Laurence Olivier. She is also remembered for her colorful personal life. Oberon was mixed-race, and grew up in India at a difficult time. She had a complex family history hidden beneath a convoluted origin story she passed off as fact on her way to stardom. Oberon met Wolders while making her final film, *Interval* (1973) – she played an aging beauty falling for a handsome young artist. The co-stars brought their roles from the reel to reality, as they fell in love and married in spite of a 25-year age gap. She passed away in late 1979. Her widower, Wolders, would thereafter become the love of another brunette beauty's life.

Hepburn and Wolders met at a party. He had asked her out to dinner, but she said she had a shooting schedule. Wolders would later say he thought he was being gently rebuffed, but afterwards, she would be the one to issue him an invitation. They had great chemistry almost immediately, and he would be her companion from 1980 to her death in 1993. They never took that walk down the aisle, but they always considered themselves unified as if in marriage.

Hepburn and Wolders were a mature couple who found each other relatively late in life but to them, the timing was perfect. They were in their 40's but still so beautiful, and many of their publicly available photographs would show them in gowns and tuxedos in the cosmopolitan set's hottest ticket events. A fashion gala here, a Hollywood event there, even one with Ronald Reagan at the Gipper's White House in 1981. But it wasn't just about glamour. He joined her all over the world in her charity work too, and they had private photos at home as well, with pets and no makeup, sitting on the couch, taking a walk… moments of quiet, romantic ordinariness. He was indeed very supportive of her, even as early as 1980, when he joined her in Dublin to see her ailing father before he died. Their time together included some of the most critical moments in her private life; the passing of her father, the passing of her mother in 1985, and the marriage (though short-lived) of her eldest child, Sean, in 1985. They were also together when she received her cancer diagnosis in 1992.

Audrey Hepburn's shocking diagnosis came 12 years after she and Robert Wolders started a life together. She was the epitome of grace right up to the very end. When she was told she had a few months left to live, she reportedly feared pain, but not death. One of her final wishes was to be in Switzerland for her last Christmas, and her loving friends moved heaven and earth to grant it. At the time, her health was already in a fragile, precarious state. A normal flight would have been her undoing, so a private jet was arranged for her by her dearest pals, Hubert de Givenchy and Bunny Mellon. Shortly after Christmas, she passed away in January, 1993.

Humanitarian Work

Audrey Hepburn was a lovely woman who was generous with her heart, not only for the men she loved, not only for her family and friends, not only for the people who delighted in working with her, but also for the struggling children of the world. In 1989, she was appointed Goodwill Ambassador for UNICEF – among the first and most prominent of the celebrities to share their time and talents with the organization.

UNICEF was founded in 1946, as The International Children's Emergency Fund ("ICEF"), following the unprecedented horrors faced by children in the wake of World War II. They worked to provide aid for children's health without discrimination, regardless of politics – a policy that would bring them to such places as Vietnam, Cambodia, Sudan and Iraq, even in times of conflict. Eventually, it became a permanent agency with the United Nations, and removed "International" as well as "Emergency" from their name as their work extended not only to post-war aid and helping nations, but also to activities like eradicating preventable childhood diseases, improving water access and sanitation, providing maternity care, instituting nutrition programs, livestock training and promoting childhood literacy and education, for needy countries as well as classes like the urban poor within nations. They retained the established acronym of "UNICEF," however.

Their first celebrity "Ambassador at Large" was American entertainer, Danny Kaye, who was appointed in 1954, and he would be followed by many A-list names willing to share in UNICEF's vision of improving children's lives, anywhere in the world that they may be. Some of the most famous, international names to hold the esteemed role are pop superstar Katy Perry, sporting legends Serena Williams and David Beckham, Jordan's Queen Rania, Hong Kong crossover megastar Jackie Chan and Oscar winner and Hollywood institution, Susan Sarandon.

Audrey Hepburn was one of their most prominent ambassadors, and few could match her right to speak on behalf of innocent children caught in hardship and/or conflict. She was barely in her teens when she was living in occupied Holland during World War II, so she had firsthand experience of childhood privation. Her memories of oppression, and the gratitude she felt upon liberation as well as the simple generosity of soldiers who handed her chocolate bars, would always stay with her and would fuel her passion for humanitarian work. She would say of the organization she devoted the last years of her life to, "... *I was among those who received food and medical relief right after World War II... I have a long-standing gratitude and trust for what UNICEF does.*"

She wasn't just paying lip service. Part of a UNICEF Global Ambassador's job, is to use their fame and platforms to bring attention to certain issues, or engage with key influencers and actors to create positive change. For Audrey Hepburn in the 1980s, this meant going around the world on missions to experience and understand what is happening in troubled loca... bring the world's attention to it to... public awareness. For example, among... first trips in her new role was to Ethiopia, where she witnessed famine and draught amid civil strife. After her mission, she went around the United States, Canada and Europe, doing up to 15 interviews a day about her experiences. When she wasn't in the field, she was engaging with governments and participating in fundraising efforts, and would actually make several appearances at Congress as part of her advocacies.

She took her role – as she does any role be it in film or in real life – very seriously. She went to different countries for different programs and causes under UNICEF. She was in Turkey for a polio vaccine project, in ıg on street children

ther working on

ınking water. In

ated for education

did the same for

d in Sudan she looked

into the plight of displaced children.

She kept busy with her advocacies right up until she found out she was ill. It's been reported that she started feeling abdominal pains in 1992, which was originally thought to be some kind of infection. She continued with her work either way, keeping her commitments in Somalia. But when she returned to the United States and underwent tests, the doctors eventually gave her a cancer diagnosis. Though she would have surgery to relieve the illness, the prognosis was unpromising. The cancer was quickly ravaging her body.

Before she died, her work with children was recognized with the Presidential Medal of Freedom – the highest award the United States can give to a civilian. She was also honored by the Academy Awards of 1993 with the Jean Hersholt Humanitarian Award; the announcement was made early in January, but Audrey Hepburn died that month in her sleep, and it would be accepted on behalf by her son, Sean Hepburn-Ferrer, in April later that year.

Audrey Hepburn is part of Hollywood's most elite list – the "EGOT Club." These are artists who have achieved Emmy, Grammy, Oscar and Tony wins along the course of their careers. Over Hollywood's lengthy history, there are only about a dozen people listed here. But for a beautiful woman with an enviable collection of gifts that would eventually garner her a coveted spot in this list, it must be remembered that at the height of her success, Audrey Hepburn was willing to walk away from it all. What she really wanted to do was to focus on her family, and the few instances that could draw her back into the public eye were her humanitarian work, the occasional compelling project, and tributes or events honoring those she worked with and loved. She was a woman in the best sense of the word. She was a lover and mother, a devoted friend, a fighter for those who could not stand up for themselves, and an inspiration for others to do the same. These are probably what she would consider her greatest achievements.

Audrey Hepburn's last role on screen, a small role in Steven Spielberg's *Always* (1989), is perhaps small but extremely fitting – she had played an angel.

Audrey Hepburn's Legacy

Audrey Hepburn is big business.

People's desire to forge a connection with her raises stunning sums at auction. Items include letters, photographs, clothes, scripts, jewelry and other memorabilia. And oh, what sums these items can command. In September, 2017, her shooting script of *Breakfast at Tiffany's* went for almost $850,000 at auction. Through online and live sales through London auction house Christie's, various items, including the said script, some jewelry, photos and (*of course!*) clothing, picked up over $6 million. The auction was made possible by her two sons, who wanted their mother's things to be able to fetch funds for her charitable causes, as well be put into the hands of people who continue to adore and appreciate her.

The guardians of Audrey Hepburn's name and likeness – her powerful brand - are Sean Hepburn-Ferrer, her only child from her first marriage with Mel; and Luca Dotti, her only child from her second marriage with Dr. Andrea Dotti. Any child may perhaps be considered the carrier of their parent's legacy, but in the case of these men and their late superstar mother, it is also a living. Audrey Hepburn, after all, has a seriously lucrative posthumous career.

Audrey Hepburn's name and likeness, still sells. It's not just about things she actually owned and touched while she was alive, as in the case of the items that have gone for auction. Decades after her most iconic works, and decades after her death, Audrey Hepburn's star still shines and is effective for use in advertising. Her very image, conveys beauty and style, yes, but more importantly, powerful femininity, class, and timeless grace. Her images appear for luxury timepiece brand Longines, accompanied by the copy, "*Elegance is an attitude.*" Her likeness was recreated in 2014 for a stunning and surprisingly lifelike Dove Chocolate / Galaxy television ad, asking, "*Why have cotton when you can have silk?*" In 2006, a Gap campaign to "*Keep it Simple*" included a TV commercial featuring clips of Audrey from *Funny Face*, to advertise the clothing company's classic, skinny black pants.

These are just a few of the ads that use her name and trademark image, whereas others settle for an invocation of her, through key elements of her iconic style. Fashion and entertainment magazines are particularly fond of doing this, dressing up today's stars in Audrey Hepburn-style garb, hair and makeup. Actress, comedian and bestselling writer Tina Fey appeared on the cover of *Entertainment Weekly* in full, Holly Golightly glory – LBD, elbow-length gloves, chignon, tiara, pearls, long cigarette holder and oh yes, a Cat. In 2006, Academy Award-winning actress, Natalie Portman, wore the original black Givenchy piece for a *Harper's Bazaar* cover. Another Academy Award-winning beauty, Anne Hathaway, channeled the icon in a shoot for *Vogue*.

These are, of course, by design. Sometimes, even when they don't intend to do it, comparisons to Audrey Hepburn are inevitable whenever a beautiful, young, stylish, elfin, waifish actress of some caliber and gravitas catches the world's attention. Natalie Portman, Emma Watson and Lily Collins all got that treatment. It's almost as if the world misses her terribly, and is in constant search for that Audrey Hepburn spirit in every promising actress who comes our way.

But there's simply more to Audrey Hepburn than meets the eye and that is probably why "the new" or "the next" Audrey is so hard to find. It is a spirit, a sense of something deeper and larger and more fundamental, but all the same something difficult to grasp and articulate. She was an Original. She had It, that X-factor, that strange, secret appeal.

Maybe it came from the vulnerabilities carved by her childhood – broken family, walkout father, parents who were not openly affectionate. Maybe it came from her experiences of war – the act she had to put up to help the Resistance, the secrets she had to keep to survive in an occupied country, the hunger and privation she had to suffer, the violence she saw on the streets, the homes she had to abandon in search of safety. Maybe it came from her failed relationships. Either way, all of these things came together to form a singular, profoundly appealing and unforgettable woman. All these hardships somehow made her strong and lovely and delightful, as if a series of wrongs could make a right.

If anyone can package that quality and sell it, they would be breaking the bank. In the meantime, it hasn't hurt companies to try, and they use invocations of her or her actual, trademarked image, to attempt to sell their goods and services. And make no mistake – her name is a brand and can in certain contexts, actually, *actually* come with a trademark sign.

The commercialization of her image has met with some criticism from certain purists and fans. It cheapens her likeness, some would say. She was a private person and so elegant and tasteful. Should you really have her image peddle chocolate and pants? How would she feel about that? Indeed, the protection of her image and legacy had even courted a recent set of controversies.

In 2017, there would be suits between her son, Sean Ferrer, and the charity established in her name. There were issues of who had unlimited rights to the use of the Audrey

Hepburn intellectual property, with or without the necessity of Sean and brother Luca's permissions. There were allegations that Sean had been interfering in their work, potentially damaging his own mother's reputation. Later that same year, Sean would be raising complaints of his own too, contesting that control and rights fell upon him and his brother as principal heirs, and expressing disapproval with how the some of the fund's activities went against Audrey's charitable intentions, including high administrative costs and executive salaries as well as insufficient percentages of proceeds used in charity work. These are just the barest details of the complaints and suits. It's a complex issue going into ownership of IP, and limitations on who and what can be used for what purpose, and how proceeds are to be spent.

Everyone just wants to be protective of Audrey Hepburn's legacy, and all claim to be selective in the use of her image and where they may appear and what they sell and stand for. Hopefully it is settled in the best possible way, not only for the preservation of Audrey Hepburn's image, but also for the children's charities that the fund - named for her and established by those who love her - supports. After all, for good or ill, her image still creates proceeds of which a large part is channeled into the Audrey Hepburn Children's Fund – and this is probably what would be most important for a humanitarian like Audrey Hepburn.

50079001R00055

Made in the USA
Columbia, SC
31 January 2019